Life Ablaze

Life Ablaze
A Woman's Novena

Joan Chittister, O.S.B.

Franklin, Wisconsin
with
Benetvision
Erie, Pennsylvania

An apostolate of the Priests of the Sacred Heart, a Catholic religious congregation, the mission of Sheed & Ward is to publish books of contemporary impact and enduring merit in Catholic Christian thought and action. The books published, however, reflect the opinion of their authors and are not meant to represent the official position of the Priests of the Sacred Heart.

2000

Sheed & Ward
7373 South Lovers Lane Road
Franklin, Wisconsin 53132
1-800-266-5564

Benetvision
355 East Ninth Street
Erie, PA 16503-1107
814-459-5994
Fax: 814-459-8066
msbpr@juno.com
www.erie.net/~erie-osb

Printed in the United States of America

Cover and interior design by Madonna Gauding
Cover art by Michael O'Neill McGrath, OSFS

Scripture quotations are from the New Revised Standard Version of the Bible, copyright 1989 by the Division of Christian Education of the National Council of the Churches of Christ in the USA. Used by permission. All rights reserved.

Life Ablaze: A Woman's Novena, originally published by Benetvision, Erie, PA 1997.

Library of Congress Cataloging-in-Publication Data

Chittister, Joan.
    Life ablaze : a woman's novena / Joan D. Chittister.
        p. cm.
    ISBN 1-58051-041-8 (pbk. alk. paper)
    1.   Catholic women—Prayer-books and devotions—English. I. Title.

BX2170.W7 C45 2000
242'.643—dc21

99-051454

Contents

INTRODUCTION

Novenas, nine consecutive days of prayer, are an honored and revered tradition in the Church. They echo the nine days of prayer that Mary and the apostles spent together, shocked by the second loss of Jesus at the Ascension and so doubly confused about what they were to do in the future. They were praying for the Holy Spirit.

"If I do not go away," Jesus said, "the Advocate will not come" (John 16:7). But Jesus did go and the Advocate—the Holy Spirit, the presence of God with us—did come, calling courageous women before us to greatness and strength far beyond even their own expectations.

That same Holy Spirit lives in us, today, guiding our hearts and leading our minds to deal well with the life in which we find ourselves. The gifts of the Holy Spirit—wisdom, fortitude, understanding, knowledge, piety, fear of the Lord, and counsel—are breathed into our souls by the Holy Spirit.

It is then the presence of the Holy Spirit for which we must pray as we face the challenges and burdens of our own lives, knowing that, as the Spirit called women before us to feats unheard of, that same Spirit now calls us.

Traditionally, novenas are prayed in preparation for a special feast or for a special intention. This woman's novena may be an especially powerful preparation for feasts of women: Marian feasts, the feasts of women celebrated in this novena, the birthday of a woman you know—your own birthday. It may be used to prepare for special times or events in life: for commitment ceremonies, before the birth or baptism of a child, beginning a new ministry, entering a new decade or phase of life, moving to a new home. This woman's novena may be used to connect us more deeply to earth events: the planting of a new garden, in thanksgiving for harvest, at the summer or winter solstice, when we travel into different geographical areas and cultures, at times of uncertainty, newness, and confusion. For a woman, novenas can also echo the nine months of pregnancy—the special period of waiting, hoping, preparing.

It is important to remember what novenas are still about—not the achievement of magical resolutions of life but the seeking of the Spirit, whatever form that takes. Novenas are a time to become immersed in prayer for the Spirit, a special time of fullness of life, of preparation for new life, of insights into the present one. This novena calls a woman to womanliness in the Spirit. It calls her to the fullness of the spiritual life.

Part I

The Gifts of the Spirit

WISDOM

FORTITUDE

UNDERSTANDING

KNOWLEDGE

PIETY

FEAR OF THE LORD

COUNSEL

BREATH OF THE SPIRIT

Anna, the Prophetess

LIFE

Anna, a prophetess of the Temple, is one of the first women mentioned in the New Testament. All her adult years have been spent in pursuit of the spiritual life and in tune with the spirit of God. When the child Jesus is brought by Mary and Joseph to the Temple for presentation, according to Jewish law, it is Anna who recognizes and announces him to the world. Simeon praises God for having lived to see Jesus the Messiah, but it is in Anna—through Anna—however, that the Holy Spirit speaks first to the world about Jesus: "At that moment," Scripture reads, "she came, and began to praise God and to speak about the child to all who were looking for the redemption of Jerusalem" (Luke 2:38). The voice of a woman makes Jesus known in the Temple. The Breath of the Spirit lives in her.

LESSON

Anna, a woman eighty-four years old, rises up out of the Gospels to make the link between the spirituality of women and the power of the Holy Spirit in them. The spiritual power and gifts of women are needed in both the world and the Church if the Messiah is to be fully recognized in our own time as well. Anna, apparently frail— thought to be failing—spends her last breath speaking publicly in the Temple, in exactly that place where a woman's voice could not be heard, about the presence and wonder of God. The grace of God comes regardless of sex, regardless of the prohibitions to its power. Filled with the Breath of the Spirit, no woman has the right to do less.

Intercession

Compassionate God, give us the courage of Anna to speak from our hearts to our own times about the presence of God in the world around us so that Christ may finally be fully proclaimed. May the Breath of the Spirit fill us with courage and conviction so that the wisdom of women—created by God and aflame with Jesus—may come to fullness in our world.

Prayer

Give me, **Great God**, a sense of the Breath of the Spirit within me as I . . . *(state the situation in your own life at this time for which you are praying)*.

day two

WISDOM

Catherine of Siena
(1347–1380)

LIFE

If social standards become the measure, Catherine Benincasa was an unlikely saint. Whatever the norms of the period, Catherine eschewed them. She lived a life of contemplation in her own home and organized a group of women to walk with her through the streets of Siena caring for the forgotten poor and sick—when no public services existed to provide that kind of care.

In a society in which the unmarried woman was, at least, a disappointment, if not a scandal,

Catherine had the wisdom to follow her own path—distinct from the forms approved by either the Church or the society of her period. She took an active interest in public affairs and spoke her mind about them. When, in the midst of political turmoil and division in the Church, the pope left Italy for the protection and security of the French court, Catherine argued against the move publicly and went straight to the pope himself to convince him to return.

Catherine's life makes it impossible for a woman to ignore the topics of the time on the grounds that such things are "not for women."

Lesson

Wisdom is the ability to see under the obvious to the essential meaning of any event. When we become mired in the specifics of the day—the shopping, the bookkeeping, the details of dailiness—and miss the meaning in it all, we give our souls over to the mundane in life. We lose a vision of the real importance of our lives. We lose heart.

Pray always for the wisdom it takes to rise above the irritations of the obvious to enter the soft center of the world's soul.

INTERCESSION

Loving God, grant us the wisdom of Catherine of Siena to see the place of our very simple lives in the pattern of life and the cosmic vision of your love for all of humankind. Give us the insight of Catherine of Siena so that we may walk the way of your will, whatever the cost, whatever the questions. Give us the graces we need to bring new life to dull days, new faith to darkness, new hope in the face of heavy burdens.

PRAYER

Give me, **Great God**, a sense of the Breath of the Spirit within me as I . . . (*state the situation in your own life at this time for which you are praying*).

FORTITUDE

Joan of Arc
(1412–1431)

LIFE

Joan of Arc is a young woman's hero and an older woman's hope. She lived in a period of political turmoil and Church division—when England wanted France, France suffered from feudal rivalries, and the Church struggled with nationalism in its own ranks. Into the midst of such fury came a young woman who heard God's voice in her heart calling her to restore France to the French and save a people under siege from the incessant English-French struggle that came to be known in history as The Hundred Years' War.

In the end, captured and turned over to the English, Joan was burned at the stake by one Church court, despite the fact that she had been endorsed by another. Hers is a bitter story of betrayal, political rivalries, and idealism in conflict with politics. "I would rather die than revoke what God has made me do," she told her inquisitors at the trial that pronounced her heretic and ordered her burned at the stake.

Lesson

Joan of Arc is a woman with a conscience, a woman with a mission. She is a woman who is bold enough to claim that she has access to God and that God has outrageous plans for her. She is a woman who threatens the status quo. Joan is not welcome in polite circles, but her fortitude, her ability to perdure under stress, and her commitment to do right in the midst of horrendous wrong mark her as a woman of grace. They managed to kill Joan, yes, but they could not damp her spirit.

Intercession

God of Strength, may the spirit of fortitude that filled Joan of Arc fill the women of our day as well so that your will may come to pass whatever the situation and wherever the evil that seeks to deter it. Give us the courage to persist in the face of defeat and to continue in the face of weariness so that what you will for creation may, in the end, triumph over lesser goals.

Prayer

Give me, **Great God**, a sense of the Breath of the Spirit within me as I . . . *(state the situation in your own life at this time for which you are praying).*

UNDERSTANDING

Teresa of Avila

(1515–1582)

LIFE

In a period of political, economic, and intellectual upheaval, Teresa of Avila brought the concerns of the soul to new heights. She made contemplation, mysticism, and union with God things to be sought in everyday life. She brought understanding to piety. She wed the physical and the spiritual dimensions of life into one great walk with God. "We aren't angels," she taught emphatically. "We've got bodies." The point was clear: The spiritual life was normal; the normal was spiritual. Teresa was declared the first woman

Doctor of the Church—in 1970—over fifty years after John of the Cross, her disciple, was named doctor. Teresa teaches what many have yet to learn: Women have a place as teachers of the faith, directors of souls, and models of the spiritual life.

LESSON

The gift of understanding is given to us so that we can come to see the ideas under the ideas that direct our lives. Understanding gives us a look at the long view, the "God's-eye" view of things—allowing us to see meaning and order in what could otherwise appear to be chaos. Teresa of Avila brought understanding to questions of spiritual development and human life. As a result, she fired human souls to reach for God in new ways. The gift of understanding enables all of us to live life with depth and purpose so that every moment of life can be lived to the center of the soul.

Intercession

God of Mystery and Presence, fill us with the understanding of your presence in our souls so that whatever life demands of us may become for us the stuff of union and the grist of growth in you. Give us, too, an awareness of your presence in the darkest moments of life so that, filled with you, no deprivation can possibly leave us destitute.

Prayer

Give me, Great God, a sense of the Breath of the Spirit within me as I . . . *(state the situation in your own life at this time for which you are praying).*

KNOWLEDGE

Hildegard of Bingen
(1098–1179)

LIFE

Hildegard of Bingen was born in the Rhineland and was promised to God in religious profession at birth. But she was no ordinary novice from a wealthy medieval family. She was unusually spiritual, uncannily brilliant, and formidably strong. Hildegard was a writer, a musician, a scientist, a preacher, and a religious visionary. She compiled encyclopedias, reported intellectual visions, preached church reform, and acted as director to many of the heads of Europe.

Hildegard brought knowledge to good will.

She didn't simply talk charming talk; rather, she studied the great ideas of the time, wrestled with the great questions of the age, and approached all of them with clarity of soul and depth of mind. She understood what others never even thought to question, and she wrote her vision of life, cosmology, creation, and grace in treatises on the spiritual life. She scolded kings and confronted bishops who attempted to bring her spirit under the yoke of a lesser law than the one inscribed in her heart by the God whose mind she plumbed for Truth and Justice.

LESSON

The spiritual life is about more than piety or regular adherence to religious practices. To be truly spiritual we must, as Benedict of Nursia counsels in his ancient monastic Rule, give ourselves over to the "school of the Lord's service." We need to bring knowledge to virtue so that our spirituality does not become bad theology. A commitment to knowledge is what provides us with the tools we need to make judgments that are true and kind, compassionate and just. The knowledge of God makes us free of the kind of guilt and scrupulosity, compulsion and righteousness, that tempt us to put more effort into maintaining institutions than plumbing God's mysteries in our own lives.

Intercession

God of Truth and God of Beauty, seed in us, as in Hildegard, a knowledge of good and evil so that, knowing one from the other, we may grow in passion for good and in awareness of evil. Give us the mind to bring knowledge to others and the heart to say the truth under all circumstances. Give us a love for the intellectual life and the stamina to pursue it so that, filled with your truth, we may never become enamored of anything less in life.

Prayer

Give me, **Great God**, a sense of the Breath of the Spirit within me as I . . . *(state the situation in your own life at this time for which you are praying).*

day six

PIETY

Elizabeth Lange
(c.1800)

LIFE

Catholic immigrants knew the burden of discrimination and prejudice that came with being a minority in a Protestant country in the early years of United States' history. Black Catholics knew worse: They suffered at the hands of not only Protestant zealots but also racist Catholics. Elizabeth Lange, a Cuban refugee whose father may have been white but whose mother was decidedly black, was a Catholic "woman of color" when neither white Catholics nor Protestants accepted her.

In Baltimore, Maryland, a "border" state between the slave-holding South and the industrial North, black children had no security at all—not the plantation system of the South, harsh as it may have been, or the opportunities of the North, with its dependence on education for advancement. Elizabeth Lange, scorned by white priests, resented by white parishioners, and questionable to white bishops, set out full of a piety that brooks no obstacles to follow the Law above the law, to found a religious community of black sisters to educate black children. Without chaplains, donations, or educational support in a system that did not allow blacks to attend Catholic colleges until 1924—when Villanova in Philadelphia admitted its first black students—Elizabeth confronted a system that saw no reason to provide schools for domestic laborers who, it was said, had "neither souls to be saved nor minds to be instructed."

And she did it.

Lesson

Despite every obstacle, Elizabeth Lange's Oblate Sisters of Providence thrived, with no thanks, with little help, and with a great deal of difficulty. They were a silent shame, a vibrant voice to us all. They were ecumenical, independent, and brave beyond telling. They were women who knew their own mind and their place in the Church long before it was a question to anyone else. They were pious women for whom piety was an impelling fire, not an excuse to ignore the social sins around them. Today, they are witnesses to the white community of what Christianity is really all about.

Intercession

God of Africa, African God, give to white hearts a sense of color and people of color the grace to forgive whites their sins. As women, give us whatever new piety it takes to do justice in an unjust world, to look beyond the social castes and classes and categories, designed to keep some people up by putting other people down, to form the community you made us to be. Give us the heart of Elizabeth Lange to persevere beyond humiliation and rejection to that point in life where all your gifts come alive in us.

PRAYER

Give me, Great God, a sense of the Breath of the Spirit within me as I . . . *(state the situation in your own life at this time for which you are praying).*

FEAR OF THE LORD

Kateri Tekakwitha

(1656–1680)

LIFE

Kateri Tekakwitha was the child of an Algonquin mother and an Iroquois father. The Algonquins were a conservative, contemplative people, a nomadic people who foraged for what they needed to live and amassed little. There was a stoicism about them, a communion with the Great Spirit that gave them both depth and endurance. The Iroquois, on the other hand, were a strong, warlike, even cruel, agricultural people, among whom the ability to bear pain was held in high esteem. Even the children of the tribe competed with one another in their ability to tolerate suffering.

Kateri, impelled by "fear of the Lord," was a blend of both traditions: prayerful and contemplative like the Algonquin, strong and stoic like the Iroquois. Both qualities she brought to her life as a Christian.

Kateri Tekakwitha rejected the dissolute life spawned among the Indians by the French fur traders who paid for pelts in liquor, and she brought to the white world proof of the spiritual maturity of the Indian personality. Indians, for instance, were not permitted to receive holy Communion for at least two years after their conversion, for fear they were, by nature, unable to live the faith. Kateri's life, however, made this policy suspect. She lived a pious life and devoted herself to the theology of the cross. She chose to be a dedicated virgin despite the fact that the Church denied Indian women the right to live a religious life. Each of those qualities was a sign of contradiction to Indian and Europeans alike. To the Indians, she presented a life of self-control and penance to rival the feats of the bravest of warriors. To the Europeans, she presented an Indian who was far holier than they. After all, whites reasoned, if Indians were "savage" and only half-souled, how could they possibly be saintly? But she was—and by their own standards. Kateri's mind grasped the glory of God and lived in the awe of it.

LESSON

Fear of the Lord is an ancient spiritual concept meant not to inspire anxiety, guilt, or dread of God, but to describe what happens to the soul that lives in the awareness of the glory of God. To pray for fear of the Lord is to pray for an abiding consciousness of God's presence in us. Fear of the Lord draws us like a magnet, turns our lives inside out, and makes all the rough ways smooth. Fear of the Lord gives us the kind of courage that comes from knowing, as the poet said, that "God and I are a majority."

Intercession

Fill us, **Gentle God**, with so great a sense of you in our souls that we never know abandonment, never know despair. Lead us beyond ourselves to become what of you we were born to be. Never let us be deterred by those who burden us with false expectations. At the same time, never let us succumb to the diminishment that comes from being denied the hope of achieving any expectations at all. Give us the unremitting energy that comes from a piety built on the discovery in ourselves of the wonder of you.

Prayer

Give me, **Great God**, a sense of the Breath of the Spirit within me as I . . . *(state the situation in your own life at this time for which you are praying).*

COUNSEL

Dorothy Day

(1897–1980)

LIFE

Dorothy Day was a searcher who went from agnosticism to Catholicism, an American who went from communism to socialism, a woman who went from a live-in partner to celibacy, a revolutionary who went from the thought of violent revolution to a total commitment to nonviolence. Dorothy Day was a woman open to learning, open to change.

Dorothy Day spent her life speaking peace in a world more comfortable with waging war than with doing the hard work of justice. She identified with the poor she served in soup kitchens and shelters for the homeless. She went to jail to get the vote for women and to bring the world to consciousness about the sins of nuclearism. And through it all, Dorothy taught us and taught us and taught us about the goodness of God and the evils of any system that develops one part of itself at the expense of the other. In her, the virtue of counsel lived again. She lived well with the great questions of life and set out to teach the rest of us to do the same.

Lesson

The gift of counsel is the gift of spiritual search. Unless we are willing to take and give counsel, unless we are intent on pursuing questions with a seeker's heart, we run the risk of going through life trapped in the narrow confines of our own experiences, our own limited opportunities, our own measured view of the world, and our own personal capacity for knowledge. What we learn from what we see and hear and read around us comes to us as a gift of the

Holy Spirit. Dorothy Day models for all of us the power of a pilgrim's heart. Just when we have decided that we know everything there is to know, someone clones a sheep, finds another comet, maps another gene. All I know for sure is that God is in creation; it is for us to listen hard enough to hear God's voice there.

INTERCESSION

God of Life, open our minds and hearts to the voice of life around us so that we can receive the counsel you send and give to others the counsel we ourselves have learned. Bring us home to your Word in everything we do. Give us the grace to ask the right questions and the heart to recognize the right answers. Let us cease to live in fear of the unknown, trusting always that the possibilities of creation are all paths to you.

Prayer

Give me, Great God, a sense of the Breath of the Spirit within me as I . . . *(state the situation in your own life at this time for which you are praying).*

day nine

THE FIRE OF THE SPIRIT

Mary Magdalene

LIFE

Mary Magdalene is one of the most misidentified people in Scripture. She is not, for instance, the "woman of the city who was a sinner." How do we know? Because Luke is the Evangelist who introduces both—one in 7:36–50 and the other immediately afterwards in 8:1–3.

Mary Magdalene is one of the women disciples of Jesus. She is one of the women philanthropists who support Jesus "out of their own resources." Mary Magdalene is important enough to be called by name, an uncommon thing for women in male documents and ancient societies. She is mentioned more times than any other woman in the New Testament, except Mary the mother of Jesus. Mary Magdalene recognizes Jesus early in his ministry and follows him all the way to the cross. She is a completely new kind of woman—the first woman minister, a leader, a sign to women everywhere of Jesus' message within them.

LESSON

Women are not marginal to the life and ministry of Jesus. They carry the fire of the Holy Spirit into places where they are not welcome, doing things they have not done before. They go on faith in Jesus alone, and they live in trust of Jesus alone. They bear Jesus in their bodies, carry him in their hearts, speak him with their lives, and defy every system, every custom, every tradition, and every institution to do it. Then, they leave the fire to us to do the same.

May the gifts of the Holy Spirit bring fire to the earth so that the presence of God may be seen in a new light, in new places, in new ways. May our own hearts burst into flame so that no obstacle, no matter how great, may ever obstruct the message of God within them. May we come to trust the Word of God in our hearts, to speak it with courage, to follow it faithfully, and to fan it to flame in others. May the Jesus who filled women with his Holy Spirit fill the world and the Church with new respect for its power and presence.

Give me, Great God, a sense of the Breath of the Spirit within me as I . . . *(state the situation in your own life at this time for which you are praying).*

Part II

Life Ablaze

PRAYERS OF HOLY WOMEN

A LITANY OF WOMEN
FOR THE CHURCH

PRAYERS OF HOLY WOMEN

Be not lax in celebrating.
Be not lazy in the festive service of God.
Be ablaze with enthusiasm.
Let us be an alive, burning offering
Before the altar of God.

Hildegard of Bingen

Let nothing disturb thee
Let nothing frighten thee
Everything is changing
God alone is changeless.
Patience attains the goal
One who has God lacks nothing
God alone fills all our needs.

Theresa of Avila

Magnificat
(see Luke 1:42–45)

I sing your praises, God, with all my heart,
and I rejoice in you, O God of life,
for you have looked upon my lowliness
and who am I to merit your attention.

I may henceforth regard myself as happy
because you have done great things for me.
And every generation gives assent
for you are God and your name is holy.

You give your grace anew in every age
to those who live in reverence all their lives.
Grace is your strength,
but you unmask all pride;
you strip us bare of our self-conceit.

Dethroned are those who hold authority,
and poor and humble people you uphold.
You give in great abundance to the hungry
and send the rich away with empty hands.

Your people Israel you have remembered,
for mercy has been sent to all the faithful,
just as you promised to those before us,
to Abraham, to Sarah, their children forever.

(Translation by Mary David Callahan, O.S.B
© Benedictine Sisters of Erie)

All shall be well.
And all shall be well.
And all manner of things shall be well.

Julian of Norwich

I cannot dance, O God, unless you lead me.
If you will that I leap joyfully,
you must yourself first dance and sing!

Then will I leap for love.
Then will I soar from love to knowledge,
from knowledge to fruition,
from fruition to beyond all human sense.
And there I will remain
and circle forevermore.

Mechtild of Magdeburg

Keep us, O God, from all pettiness.
Let us be large in thought, in word, in deed.
Let us be done with fault-finding
and leave off all self-seeking.
May we put away all pretense
and meet each other face to face,
without self-pity and without prejudice.
May we never be hasty in judgment,
and always generous.
Let us always take the time for all things,
and make us grow calm, serene, and gentle.
Teach us to put into action our better impulses,
to be straightforward and unafraid.
Grant that we may realize
that it is the little things of life
that create differences,
that in the big things of life
we are as one.
And, O God, let us not forget to be kind.

Queen Mary Stuart

I should like a great lake of beer for the God of Hosts.
I should like the angels of Heaven
     to be drinking it through time eternal.
I should like flails of penance at my house.
I should like the men and women of Heaven
     at my house;
I should like barrels of peace at their disposal;
I should like vessels of charity for distribution;
I should like for them cellars of mercy.
I should like cheerfulness to be in their drinking.
I should like Jesus to be there among them.
I should like the three Marys of illustrious renown
     to be with us.
I should like the people of Heaven, the poor,
     to be gathered around us from all parts.

St. Bridget

A Litany of Women for the Church

Dear God, creator of women in your own image,
born of a woman in the midst of a world half women,
carried by women to mission fields around the globe,
made known by women to all the children of the earth,
give to the women of our time
    the strength to persevere,
    the courage to speak out,
    the faith to believe in you beyond
    all systems and institutions
so that your face on earth
    may be seen in all of its beauty,
so that men and women
    become whole,
so that the Church
    may be converted to your will in everything and
    in all ways.

We call on the holy women
who went before us,
channels of your Word
in testaments old and new,
to intercede for us
so that we might be given the grace
to become what they have been
for the honor and glory of God.

Saint Esther,
who pleaded against power
for the liberation of the people,

—Pray for us

Saint Judith,
who routed the plans of men
and saved the community,

—Pray for us

Saint Deborah,
lay woman and judge,
who led the people of God,

—Pray for us

Saint Elizabeth of Judea,
who recognized the value
of another woman,

—Pray for us

Saint Mary Magdalene,
minister of Jesus,
first evangelist of the Christ,

—Pray for us

Saint Scholastica,
who taught her brother, Benedict,
to honor the spirit above the system,

—Pray for us

Saint Hildegard,
who suffered interdict
for the doing of right,

—Pray for us

Saint Joan of Arc,
who put no law
above the law of God,

—Pray for us

Saint Clare of Assisi,
who confronted the pope
with the image of woman as equal,

—*Pray for us*

Saint Julian of Norwich,
who proclaimed for all of us
the motherhood of God,

—*Pray for us*

Saint Thérèse of Lisieux,
who knew the call to the priesthood
in herself,

—*Pray for us*

Saint Catherine of Siena,
to whom the pope listened,

—*Pray for us*

Saint Teresa of Avila,
who brought women's gifts
to the reform of the Church,

—*Pray for us*

Saint Edith Stein,
who brought fearlessness to faith,

—*Pray for us*

Saint Elizabeth Seton,
who broke down boundaries
between lay women and religious
by wedding motherhood and religious life,

—*Pray for us*

Saint Dorothy Day,
who led the Church
to a new sense of justice,

—*Pray for us*

✳   ✳   ✳

Mary, mother of Jesus,
who heard the call of God and answered,

—*Pray for us*

Mary, mother of Jesus,
who drew strength from the woman Elizabeth,

—*Pray for us*

Mary, mother of Jesus,
who underwent hardship bearing Christ,

—Pray for us

Mary, mother of Jesus,
who ministered at Cana,

—Pray for us

Mary, mother of Jesus,
inspirited at Pentecost,

—Pray for us

Mary, mother of Jesus,
who turned the Spirit of God
into the body and blood of Christ,

—Pray for us

Amen